This library edition published in 2012 by Walter Foster Publishing, Inc.
Distributed by Black Rabbit Books.
P.O. Box 3263 Mankato, Minnesota 56002

Designed and published by Walter Foster Publishing, Inc.
Walter Foster is a registered trademark.

Printed in Mankato, Minnesota, USA by CG Book Printers, a division of Corporate Graphics.

First Library Edition

Library of Congress Cataloging-in-Publication Data

Watch me draw Tiggerific tales / illustrated by the Disney Storybook
Artists ; step-by-step drawing illustrations by Elizabeth T. Gilbert. --
First Library Edition.
    pages cm
  ISBN 978-1-936309-87-0
 1. Animals in art--Juvenile literature. 2. Cartoon
characters--Juvenile literature. 3. Drawing--Technique--Juvenile
literature. 4. My friends Tigger & Pooh (Television program)--Juvenile
literature. I. Gilbert, Elizabeth T., illustrator. II. Disney Storybook
Artists, illustrator.
  NC1764.8.A54W39 2012
  741.5'1--dc23
                                  2012004734

052012
17679

9 8 7 6 5 4 3 2 1

WATCH ME DRAW

My Friends Tigger & Pooh

Tiggerific Tales

Illustrated by the Disney Storybook Artists
Step-by-Step Drawing Illustrations by Elizabeth T. Gilbert
Designed by Shelley Baugh • Project Editor/Writer: Rebecca J. Razo

Where can Roo, Tigger, and Pooh learn about birds, earthworms, and flowers and such? "I've got it!" says Tigger. "We can look at Darby's stupenderous book of facts!"

Draw the hummingbird!

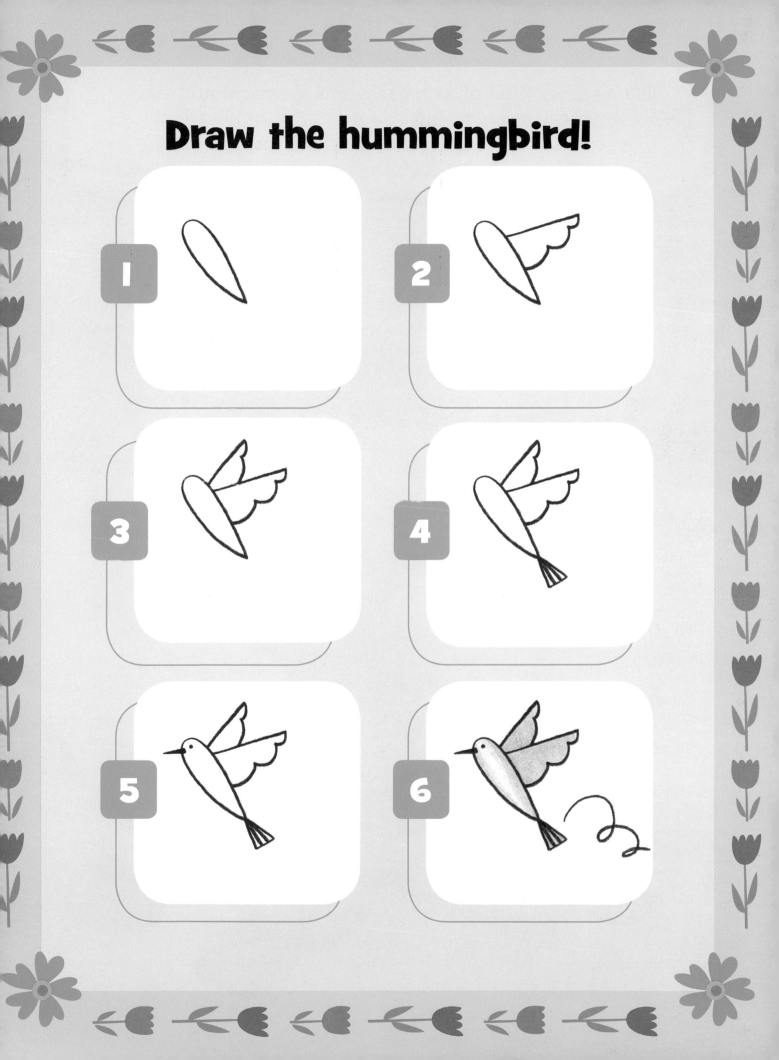

It's a snowy kind of day. Darby and Buster would like a mystery to solve, but so far they've only caught snowflakes on their tongues! That's just fine with Buster—he likes riding on the sled, too!

Draw the pine tree!

These best friends are on a tiggerific picnic.
"I like fruit," says Pooh. "But where's the honey?"
"I'm absoposilutely certain that there's a honey pot cloud in the sky!" says Tigger.

Draw the kite!

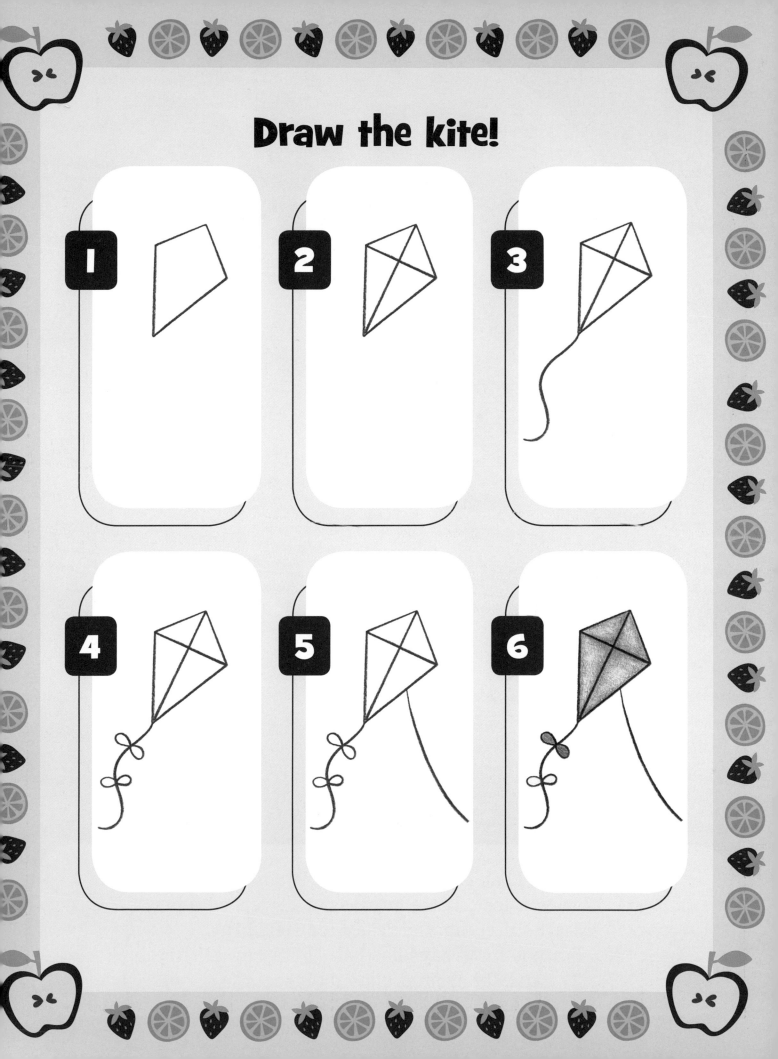

What's that flying across the moonlit sky?
"Are you lost, little guy?" asks Tigger, who is
all suited up and ready for sleuthing.
"No. I'm not lost," says the bat. "I stay up all night
and fly around chasing insects."

Draw the bat!

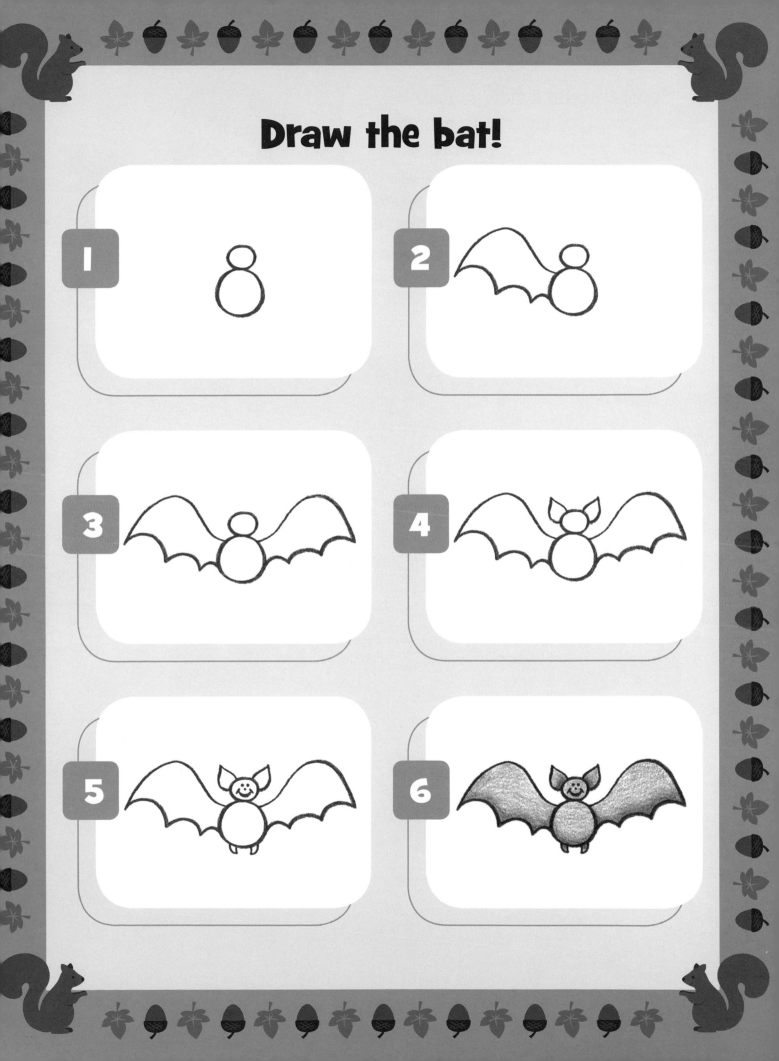

Eyore needs a new house. "Would you like to live in a house like the gopher's?" asks Darby. "Oh, I don't know," sighs Eyore. "I don't like crawling through holes in the ground." What kind of house do you think Eyore would like?

Draw the gopher!

It's a happy kind of day in the Hundred-Acre Wood. Piglet and Lumpy like to play outdoor games. Who is that jumping rope? Exackatackly! It's Roo! Another mystery is history!

Draw the snail!

"I wish I could plant honey pots instead of vegetables," says Pooh. What do you suppose Pooh planted in Rabbit's garden? Can you guess by the pictures on the signs? Think, think, think!

Draw the watering can!

Tigger and Roo are enjoying outdoor fun in the snow. Roo is using Rabbit's favorite food for the snowman's nose—do you know what it is? That was easy as peasy, wasn't it?

Draw the snowman!

"Oh bother!" says Pooh. "There are ants in my honey pots! But where did they come from?" Whoa! Sounds like another mystery! Do you know where the ants came from? Fantasterisk!

Draw the ant!

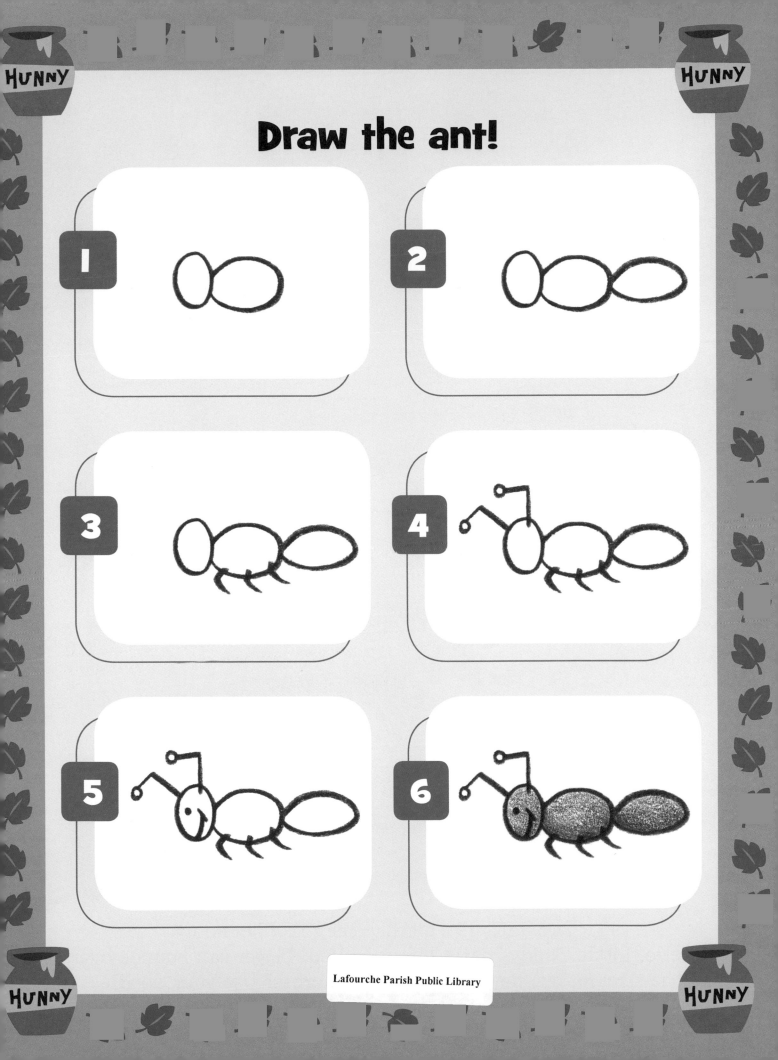

Tiggers don't like sitting—they like bouncing!
"Hello, Little Buddy!" calls Tigger to Roo. Tigger can bounce over
the stream, but how can Buster get across? Use your noodle!

Draw the butterfly!

Hooray! It's a hunnyful day! A wonderful time to put on a play! Piglet is dressed like a flowerpot and Pooh is dressed like a honeybee. Pooh loves honeybees! Can you guess why? Maybe you should ask his tummy!

Draw the honeybee!

There's no mystery that
these Super Sleuths can't solve!